Kentner

A Symposium

The editor wishes to thank Louis Kentner, Mary Shillabeer and Harold Holt Ltd for the loan of photographs; Romi Tunstall-Behrens for permission to reproduce her painting, and Terry Wilkinson for items of photographic work.

Kentner
A Symposium

Edited by Harold Taylor
Foreword by Yehudi Menuhin

Kahn & Averill, London
Pro/Am Music Resources Inc, New York

First published in 1987 by Kahn & Averill

British Library Cataloguing in Publication Data

Kentner: a symposium.
1. Kentner, Louis 2. Pianists—Great
Britain—Biography
I. Taylor, Harold, *1925–*
786.1'092'4 ML417.K5/

ISBN 0-900707-97-6

First published in the United States in 1987
by Pro/Am Music Resources, Inc.
White Plains, New York

ISBN 0-912483-11-3

Set in 11 on 13 pt Baskerville by
Input Typesetting Ltd
Printed and bound in Great Britain by
Biddles Ltd, Guildford and King's Lynn

Contents

List of Illustrations

Foreword

Louis Kentner is one of the most generously cultivated of men, for whom the sharing of life's blessings is ideally reserved for a chosen few initiates, or another chosen few awaiting initiation. He is a musician gifted with enormous talent, both creative to composer and executive – a wonderful pianist.

He is gratefully respected by the children of my School, for whom he opens ultimate doors, for he dwells in a most uncommon world, guarded behind an enigmatic smile and that envious quality of being always himself. In fact he most emphatically never wears anything on his sleeve and always appears remarkably self-sufficient and self-contained.

In a period of commercial concern for the saleability of products, his is a priceless unconcern for the 'market exigencies'. We, colleagues young and old, friends and, like myself, belonging to all these categories including that special one of brother-in-law, return to him again and again to restore contact with an authenticity largely dissipated by industrialised mass culture.

Of course, I need hardly mention he comes from Hungary – born eighty years ago in a land astonishingly rich yet fragile, in which a flowering of music and a vitality infusing all intellectual and social pursuits came quite simply and inevitably, both literally and symbolically, out of an inexhaustible soil; the same soil in fact which together with adjoining Austria nurtured the greatest musical culture of the world.

We are fortunate indeed to have with us in England a man of such rare stature, a man who has found in my dear sister-in-law, Griselda, a companion, a soul-mate (as they feel towards each other), equally bound to that quiet cultivation of spirit and the good fare which from time to time we are privileged to share. May I wish him yet many more happy returns.

Yehudi Menuhin

Preface

It is heart-warming to be able to celebrate the fact that Louis Kentner has arrived at the age of eighty with all his great qualities undimmed – not only undimmed, but actually enhanced – by the passage of time. Those of us who were fortunate enough to be present at his birthday recital at the Queen Elizabeth Hall were left in no doubt about this, as witness for one example, his nobly spacious and apparently effortless performance of Liszt's transcendental *Piano Sonata*, which re-affirmed the greatness of the work in every phrase. In another dimension, who could forget the tenderness and fine-spun magic of the little F minor *Moment Musical* of Schubert?

To close an evening which had included Beethoven's *Op 110 Sonata*, the *Four Ballades* of Chopin, the Liszt *Sonata* and two encores, he played the *Barcarolle* of Chopin, a typically generous valediction from this most generous of musicians. His ability to sustain such a huge programme is not acquired through extraordinary stamina, but by masterly economy of effort; the ways of the piano-pounding keyboard athlete are unknown to him. His hands are small for a concert pianist – fastidious hands, which appear to create the music spontaneously as they roam the keyboard in a continuous flow of supple, yet precise, gestures. His concentration is absolute; he sits very low, almost at arm's length, quietly listening, the face a mask, the eyes reduced to pinpoints. Nothing comes between him, or the audience, and the music. He has one idiosyncracy: the little blue piano stool with detachable legs which always travels with him; ordinary music stools do not wind low enough for his comfort. Yet should this be regarded as an idiosyncracy? Piano playing is a sedentary occupation, and no one demonstrates the relationship between fine sitting and fine playing more precisely than Louis Kentner.

He brings the same concentration and fineness of perception to his teaching. Whilst the pupil plays, he sits at the opposite end of the room, as if in mid-stalls at a concert, often listening with eyes closed, his involvement with the performance betrayed by his hands, which begin to make the gestures of conducting an invisible orchestra. The pupil is allowed to play the whole piece or movement without interruption and is always given an account of the general impression he has made, before the detailed work of teaching begins. This usually involves several journeys from the armchair to the piano stool and back again during the course of a lesson, for Kentner is a great believer in the virtues of demonstration and example. Readers of his book, *Piano*, will know that he has no particular technical method – he has very little faith in 'methods' – but he has a seemingly inexhaustible supply of 'tricks of the trade' for transforming the difficult into the easy. On the other hand he does not pretend that there are any short cuts available in the patient and unending search for artistic truth.

Prefaces are always written last. I have attempted to describe some visual details of the artist at work, primarily because they have not been mentioned elsewhere in this book and because I hope that they will go some way towards 'setting the stage' for the chapters which follow. I am deeply grateful to all those who have helped to paint this verbal birthday portrait of Louis Kentner as teacher, performer, composer and friend; not least to the artist himself, whose own *Sketch of a self-portrait* has added a dimension of historical interest and importance. I hope that this book will not be read solely as a eulogy, but also as a re-affirmation of certain artistic ideals which – like freedom – demand constant vigilance for their preservation in an age of high technology and low standards. Long may we continue to reap the benefits of Louis Kentner's unremitting vigilance in the service of music.

In keeping with the spirit in which this book has been compiled, any royalties accruing from sales will go to the Musicians' Benevolent Fund.

Biographical Note

Louis Kentner was born in Karwin, Silesia on the 19th July, 1905. He received his first piano lessons from his mother and was accepted at the Royal Franz Liszt Academy of Music in Budapest before he was seven years old. There he studied the piano with Arnold Szeckely, and composition with Hans Koessler, Leo Weiner and Zoltán Kodály. He gave his first recital in Budapest at the age of thirteen; three years later he made his debut in Berlin. His career has taken him round the world many times, including several tours of the Soviet Union and the United States. He settled in England in 1935 and became a British citizen in 1946.

Louis Kentner is well-known for his advocacy of the music of his fellow-countryman, Franz Liszt; but Liszt's music forms only a small part of his vast repertoire, which is drawn from many different styles and periods. He has given whole cycles of Bach's '48' preludes and fugues and the thirty two sonatas of Beethoven in many capital cities and played much music by his own contemporaries. In Hungary he gave first performances of works by Weiner, Kodály and Bartók, including the Hungarian première of Bartók's *Second Piano Concerto* under Klemperer. Since coming to England he has played all the piano music of Constant Lambert and premièred concertos by Alan Rawsthorne and Sir Michael Tippett.

Other important first performances have included the *Tryptich* for piano of Sir Arthur Bliss and the *Violin Sonata* of Sir William Walton, with Yehudi Menuhin, with whom Louis Kentner has often played and recorded. They also formed a trio with Gaspar Cassado which was a feature of many European festivals until the great Spanish 'cellist's untimely death in 1966. Louis Kentner has served on the juries of the Warsaw, Leeds, Maryland and other international piano competitions and his other activities include teaching, composing and writing. He gives regular master classes for the Yehudi Menuhin School and is the author of *Piano* (Macdonald Janes 1976). His other publications include *Three Sonatinas for Piano* (O.U.P. 1939) and contributions to *Franz Liszt – the Man and his Music* (ed. Alan Walker; Barrie and Jenkins 1970).

Louis Kentner has been President of the Liszt Society since 1965; he is also President of the Chopin Society and British President of the European Piano Teachers Association. He is an Honorary Member of the Royal Academy of Music and in 1978 he was made a Companion of the Order of the British Empire.

I Sketch of a self-portrait

Louis Kentner

I

Anyone who, like myself, was born in Central Europe before the First World War, was born in a country which has ceased to exist, or, if you prefer it, in a country which did not exist at the time of his birth. The groups of elder statesmen who in Versailles created new countries out of the ruins of the Hapsburg Empire, calling them Czecho-Slovakia, Yugoslavia and so forth, created private problems for individuals instead of solving them. Thus I have a standing reply to any suggestion that I was born in Czechoslovakia, which is geographically correct but historically wrong: "Sir, I am much older than Czechoslovakia".

My father was a man who, in earlier, less inhibited times, might have committed crimes, and hung for it.

In later years, when I read Dostoevsky's *The Brothers Karamazoff*, I was amazed to find how much Father Karamazoff had in common with my father. Alas, I am not at all like saintly Aliosha. My affinity is more with Ivan, the atheist.

However, in our soft society, where potential, as well as real criminals, are protected, encouraged and sometimes even rewarded, my father did quite well in his career; first as a railway official, later as a businessman.

It must be admitted that my father had one redeeming quality: he loved music. A bad amateur pianist, he spent hours at a bad piano, trying to read piano reductions of Puccini operas or Delibes ballets, an exercise in which his small son, myself, was ordered to take part as a page-turner. I managed to follow the printed up-and-down lines of the copy, collating them with the movements of my father's hands and the resultant sounds, and eventually, to everybody's amazement, I could read music without any tuition. Later, when I was able to stumble through some Czerny exercises, I had to play four-hand duets with my father: Beethoven symphonies and other works far beyond my, or his, powers. He insisted on counting the beats very loudly; the counting followed the playing (which was totally unrhythmical), and not the other way round. Nevertheless, I feel today, that blundering through them in this illiterate fashion, I became more familiar with some great masterpieces than others who have heard them in perfect performances on records.

As a small child, I suffered from nightmares, waking up screaming. One of these is still vivid in my memory. I dreamt that a bee stung me very near the eye. I woke in a room where a yellow light was burning, and a pair of female arms – my mother's – picked me up comfortingly. A few years later, this dream became reality: a bee – or a wasp – stung me dangerously near the eye, losing its sting (and its life) in the process.

My mother was a gentle, timid soul. She constructed for herself a kind of spiritual mouse-hole into which she retreated when my father's arrogance threatened her peace of mind. She gave me my first piano lessons, before my father took over. My mother was a migraine sufferer, and I still remember the darkened room where she lay isolated, sometimes for many days on end.

My sister was affectionate and self-effacing and, because she was not particularly talented, received an unjustly smaller share of parental care than I did; but far from resenting this, she gave me all the moral support possible to her. She was also my first pupil; I tried to teach her the piano, with less than brilliant results. At the time of writing, she is alive in Budapest.

II

When it was thought in the family that I showed talent (or promise of sorts), I was taken to the Royal Academy of Music in Budapest for the entrance examination. This was an important day in my six years' old life. (The average age of students in that institution was 17 – 18, but there was no rigid rule as to age.) I do not remember what or how I played, but I do remember that the president of the examining panel – a professor called Szendy, a pupil of Liszt – summoned me to his presence after my performance and, looking very stern, enquired: "Do you like chocolate, boy?" I answered, somewhat perplexed: "Yes, sir, I do." Thereupon he dived into his pocket, produced something brown and sticky, handed it to me and said, with a terrible frown: "We have accepted you, boy".

Now I was an academician and a schoolboy as well (I developed a passion for reading long before I was taught the alphabet), I was enjoying a new-found freedom from the oppression of home life – a life of tears, quarrels and door slamming – when an incident occured which must be mentioned because it turned out to be important for my musical evolution. A young teacher at school who taught the boys choral singing and who was in his free time a student of Kodály in composition, one day to his

utter surprise, met one of his young pupils, myself, in a corridor of the Academy. "What are you doing here?", he asked me. I said I was going to have a piano lesson, and so we were, in a way, colleagues. After this shattering discovery, there was no looking back; my new friend kept me in the empty classroom while the others were playing games outside, and taught me the rudiments of theory, the science of music. I entered into the world of intervals, tonalities, church modes, and even all the different kinds of C clef, so important for score reading. This admirable young man (whose name, alas, I never knew, indeed not to this present day) gave me so much fascinating new knowledge, that it helped me over my initial disappointment with my studies at the Academy. These consisted of a rigidly imposed diet of scales, exercises and sonatinas by Bergmuller or Kuhlau, administered by young ladies on courses of pedagogy. That was not what I expected; I expected something different, something ecstatic and transcendental: Art. Later, when I had outgrown the young ladies, Art did enter my life in a secret sort of way, of which more to follow.

III

There is nothing unusual in a young boy falling in love with his sister's best friend (she was pretty and sweet and naively anxious to add to her not too significant intellectual capital by reading and discussing masses of books, a passion which I shared with her), but perhaps it is less ordinary, in this day and age, that this first love did not lead to any natural outcome, owing to the timidity of the participants. There was not even a kiss exchanged, nor any verbal avowals. All we did was to go for long walks (I never walked so much in my life!), discussing serious topics. I gave her some piano lessons, as I did my sister, and, like my sister, she was a willing but unpromising pupil.

My problems sorted themselves out in due course, but I do not propose to go into details (like some of my elder fellow-writers of reminiscences, perhaps coveting Casanova's glories). I married too young, which – despite the fact that the lady in question was a distinguished musician – turned out to be a mistake, and was rectified by divorce about eight years later. My second wife, a beautiful, talented and angelic lady, highly musical withal, has, I am happy to say, born the negative sides of my character with a saintly tolerance to this day. She is an ideal wife – far beyond my deserts.

IV

After this glimpse into the present, I return to my growing-up period, the main theme of the previous section. The frustrating love–episode had not much effect on my musical life. The growing-up process was helped by the highly beneficent emergence of two teachers, one of whom I instantly recognised as a great man. The other also filled a need, that of removing the clumsiness and lack of lucid thinking which bedevilled my early beginnings, both as a pianist and as a composer.

I am referring to Leo Weiner and Zoltán Kodály. My piano professor did not play a big part in this drama for I soon came to unflattering conclusions about his teaching abilities, perhaps unjustly. But he was a tolerant man, and in turning away from him, I incurred his mild displeasure only, not any noisy explosion of jealousy.

Leo Weiner's was the earliest and strongest of influences on me as a musician. He was a really 'great' master–pedagogue who was also a significant creative artist, a penetrating musical intelligence, self-taught in playing the piano (which he did with a cat-like instinctive physical skill but also an inability of sustained concentration), in short, a universal musician. Such a phenomenon was entirely new to me; it created a new dimension of existing, and – what was particularly delightful – from the word go an affinity was mutually felt which excluded any possibility of resistance or rebellion on my part. I simply accepted him as the norm and model in all things musical, perhaps because of the natural affinity alluded to above which led me to follow him as if hypnotised – so it must have seemed to the world, but to me it seemed that I had found my own self. Weiner commented on this in later years. He taught me chamber music first, then composition, and finally (at my request) he heard me play the piano at regular intervals as I studied new repertoire. For this purpose he came to our house about once a week. I played my pieces, he criticised, and eventually had dinner with the family (always the same dinner, for Weiner was a gourmet but also a creature of habit).

During these evenings he often clashed with my father who invoked his judgement against me on various subjects but was disappointed because Weiner always took my part, very eloquently. Very soon, he proposed the friendly "thou" address, and the teacher–pupil relationship became a great friendship – the greatest I ever had in my life. It is not for me to criticise Weiner as a composer, nor is this the right place for it. When his *Second String Quartet* won the American Coolidge Prize, he could have moved to America and become famous and rich, but this was not in his nature, and for this stubborn "true-to-himself-in-all-things" behaviour I think admiration is due to him. His great qualities as a pedagogue were soon universally recognised, and it is a well-known fact that Hungarian musicians of any category – pianists, fiddlers, conductors, composers now inundating the world – are almost certainly ex-pupils of Leo Weiner, and proud of it.

Zoltán Kodály (who taught me theory as a second subject but subsequently advised me to quit my theory course and to become a student of composition in his class) was a very different sort of person from Leo Weiner. Where Weiner was outgoing, laughter-loving, sardonic, communicative, Kodály was slow-moving, given to few words and long silences, and had a sustained air of inviolable spirituality which had an embarrassing effect on some of his pupils (perhaps because he himself seemed to live in a perpetual state of embarrassment), and this was often misinterpreted as arrogance or simply rudeness. Kodály was basically a kind person; when he heard that the young boy that was I had a passion for long walks (sometimes all day long) in the mountains that constitute the beautiful environs of Budapest, he took me out for walks in the hills, as he shared the same passion. On these walks the conversation was seldom about music, a somewhat surprising fact when one considers the aura of unwordliness surrounding this deeply spiritual man (as I believed him to be). He gave me good, sound, practical advice on how to make a career, talked wisely about concert agents, critics, etc. How I wished, many years later, that I had taken Kodály's advice, given during those walks in the hills of Buda.

As a composer, such as I was then, he helped me greatly. His criticism was trenchant, just, never discouraging, nor affected by young pupils' tendencies. He neither approved nor disapproved of the direction they took ('right' or 'left'), nor demanded imitation of himself.

Perhaps the fact that I could not wholeheartedly admire all of his music (unlike the case of Weiner) prevented another great friendship developing, besides Kodály's awkwardness of manner. Nevertheless, I was astonished by an unprecedented act on his part. When we said goodbye, he suddenly put his arms around my neck and embraced me. This was the first time, in some forty years, that he had made a gesture which gave me any inkling that he was fond of me. Alas, it was the last time.

V

To my association with Kodály, I owe some of my early reputation for quick musical perception and exceptional memory. He was still my professor in composition, although pianistically I was already circulating under my own steam, when the idea of giving all–Kodály concerts occured to him. I was asked to present his piano music on these occasions, and not only piano music, but chamber music, the accompaniments of songs, everything in which a piano and a pianist had to figure.

These annual concerts became very successful. I gave the first public performance of the *Dances of Marosszek* (a series of melodies from the district of Marosszek, arranged by Kodály for piano) in somewhat peculiar circumstances. The authentic story is as follows: I was ordered to come to the house where the Kodálys lived, at 9 a.m. on the day of the concert. Kodály answered my ring, holding a sheet of manuscript paper in his hand – it was still wet – which he handed to me, saying: "Learn this!". Thereupon he led me into the dining-room where there was no piano. But there was a sofa for me to sit on, and I memorised the first page whilst the composer pounded away in the next room. He never composed without a piano! After a while he came to me with another wet sheet, saying: "Now learn this". By lunch-time the manuscript was finished, and I had done my memorizing. Then, at last, I went home to practise, on a piano. In the evening, at the concert (which was broadcast!), I did perform to everybody's satisfaction, and from memory. The curious thing was that it never occured to me that I was doing anything out of the ordinary, or that the task I had undertaken was 'difficult'. Kodály was aware of these aspects of the event, and in later years, when he visited me in London, he used to recall the story and ask to hear me play them again. His comment was invariably that every time he heard me perform the *Dances*, they sounded different to him, as if he had never heard them before.

I came into friendly, but never intimate, contact with Béla Bartók relatively late in life, when I was asked to give the first performance in Budapest of his *Second Piano Concerto*, and heard, to my astonishment, that it was the composer himself who had put my name forward. The background of Bartók's refusal to be his own pianist in his own concerto – notwithstanding the fact that he was a brilliant pianist – is quite interesting, and deserves a short explanation. Almost every composer, who produces in our twentieth century music expressing the soul of this century (mostly an ugly, cold and dismal soul, I am sorry to say), is unaware of any negative, repellant or tortured elements in his music; unaware even of peculiarities in it. He firmly believes that everything is clear, tidy and the most natural in the world. Such a composer is astonished when he meets with hostility from the listening public. What is to some ugly, is to him beautiful. Bartók, a case in point, could not understand why his works were rarely performed, and then not over-enthusiastically applauded. He announced bitterly that Hungarian concert audiences were barbarians, and that he would never again play in Budapest, the town where he lived. (He changed his mind later). He thought that I would be a good substitute, and that is how I came to give this performance, with Otto Klemperer conducting, and Bartók attending all rehearsals, but in complete passivity. He expressed not a single word of criticism or approval, limiting himself to dangling from time to time a little pocket metronome to check the rightness of his markings in the score. But prior to this *première* (which Bartók did not attend), I went to his house many times to prepare my part of it – discovering and eliminating many mistakes in the manuscript – and I found him charming, generous and helpful. Some years later, when he died an unhappy exile in America, Kodály said of him in a funeral speech: "Bartók was a man who fervently loved his country, but whom his country loved not".

VI

I have very pleasant memories of Otto Klemperer, the conductor who shared with me the honour of giving Bartók's *Second Piano Concerto* its first Hungarian performance. The *world première* was given by the composer a few days earlier in Frankfurt, at a public concert of the German Radio. Klemperer, an enormously tall man – so tall, in fact, that he could dispense with the conductor's rostrum and still tower above the orchestra – arrived straight off the train at our first rehearsal, in complete ignorance of the score. He found me practising the piano part in one of the rooms at the Academy, and begged – or rather, ordered – me to go on playing whilst he, nonplussed by the unexpected difficulties of the complicated score, learnt to turn the pages, this being presumably the first thing a conductor must do before a first rehearsal. Consequently the rehearsal itself was a shambles; no one, except myself and Bartók who attended, had the slightest idea of what to do with the first movement, a cruel, neo-classical, rhythmically-orientated piece in which the strings of the orchestra are silent. But Klemperer was not to be defeated. He went home and studied the score and by the next rehearsal he had mastered it. His style of dealing with the orchestra was totally old-fashioned, German, professorial and tyrannical in the extreme. If anyone dared whisper, he roared: "Ruhe!" ("Silence!"), and his natural authority, plus his stature, made any rebellious attempt at resistance impossible. His interpretations of Beethoven symphonies were of the straight "no nonsense" kind but very compelling, as if his huge frame contained a soul as big as Beethoven's, which his beat could bring to bear without verbal explanations.

For this particular concert Klemperer had commissioned from Weiner an orchestration (for huge orchestra) of Bach's monumental C major *Organ Toccata*, and the two men became friends through this brilliantly successful piece of orchestral virtuosity.

A funny episode occurred when an over-ambitious concert agent approached me with the request to help a *protègé* of his, a young gypsy fiddler, to meet and perform to Klemperer and Weiner, with a view to soliciting the help of these two influential musicians in the young man's future career. Both friends agreed to hear him play in my house, on condition that a good lunch must start the proceedings, after which they must have a lie-down. The lunch was laid on; wine flowed lavishly. The boy fiddler and his impressario arrived just as Klemperer and Weiner made themselves comfortable on two sofas, assuring the world that they were ready to listen. I offered to accompany – some concerto by Vieuxtemps or Wieniawsky – but could not hear a thing; all was drowned by the snores emanating from the two sofas occupied by the two distinguished musicians. As far as I remember, this was the end, not the beginning, of one infant prodigy's career.

VII

Soon after the Bartók event I conceived the idea of emigrating to England. This was a hard decision because many were the ties linking me with Hungary, especially with Budapest; ties of family, of friends, of affection for the place itself (Budapest was a charming town at the time, just the right size for the capital of a small country, a capital city where one could go almost anywhere on foot), plus a lazy disinclination to do anything so radical as to move to another country for good. I had tried that some years before, when, following the great unexpected success of my début in Berlin, which earned me many engagements and some new friends, I made my home there. On that occasion it was partly the galloping German inflation and partly some serious family trouble which forced me to return home, and soon after that, the beginning of the Nazi tragi-comedy put an end to any lingering hope of ever entering that country again. I did not know America, a possible alternative to England, but one with which my feelings could promise no affinity, my cultural background, temperament and aims in life all being very European. So it was England or nothing.

My entry into Britain started with a ludicrous episode. That fearsome character, the Immigration Officer, questioned me very closely on the reason for my visit. I said, not knowing the disaster I was to cause, that I had an invitation from my relations, Mr. and Mrs. P . . . . . ., to stay in their house as a guest – a half-truth, as one will see. After I had passed through Immigration, and settled down in my new home in St. John's Wood, the above-mentioned ludicrous incident started: the telephone rang and an irate Immigration Officer took me to task, for apparently I had told him an untruth. My relations, as he had found out, were not married, but "living in sin". In my embarrassment – as I hadn't known that such details were of interest to the Home Office – I stammered something to the effect that the couple in question, although unmarried as yet, were going to legalise their union in a short time. This was, of course, an invention of mine. That same afternoon, Mr. P . . . . . (who too was a foreigner) received a stern gentleman from the Home Office, who threatened him with expulsion – if the promise I gave on his behalf of a speedy marriage was not fulfilled forthwith. In a couple of weeks, the poor things were (unhappily) married, and hated me ever after. They are, of course, divorced by now, and I hope they have forgiven me.

To slough off my Hungarian skin and grow a new English one did not prove a difficult operation; new friends came to my rescue who helped me to understand anything that might have seemed strange at first. These new friends also took it upon themselves to ease my way as a pianist: three recitals were arranged to make my name known to the British public. It cannot be said that I took London by storm. The press was divided, even before it became openly hostile (this hostility being partly caused by my daring to espouse the cause of Liszt, the then *bête noir* of British critics), but through my three recitals I came to meet some admirers of Liszt who later became enthusiastic personal friends of mine. They encouraged me to give an all–Liszt recital, which proved to be the turning-point in my somewhat sluggish career. Constant Lambert, the then music critic of the *Sunday Referee* (the paper no longer exists), and a fanatical Lisztian, wrote a sensational review. Others followed suit, and so it happened – not indeed by design on my part, my favourite composers being classical or contemporary – that I was accepted as a champion of Liszt; a 'specialist'. Far be it for me to complain. Being someone on his knees to Beethoven, Bach, Schubert did not prevent me from loving Liszt too with all my heart, and the new 'label' did this for me, amongst other things: it forced me to learn a new repertoire and to improve my technique towards being adequate to playing the works of Liszt. It also helped me a little to discover in myself a latent affinity with Liszt's music. So I had to come to England, the anti-Liszt land *par excellence*, to become a Liszt player *par excellence* – a curious truth, come to think of it. It is a matter of modest satisfaction that since my arrival in England and the work of the Liszt Society, much anti-Liszt prejudice has disappeared and that I can claim a small share in this result.

VIII

Three British conductors with whom I worked in the early days left lasting impressions on me:

Sir Thomas Beecham, who gave me my first important concert engagement in England. A witty, urbane personality, he made the orchestra glow and sparkle in a series of Mozart concerto performances by the irresistable vitality of his music-making.

Sir Adrian Boult, with whom I gave the European première of Bartók's *Third Piano Concerto*; a splendid musician, under-rated because he did not impress the audience, rather than the orchestra, by the choreographic exhibitions beloved of some other conductors.

Sir Malcolm Sargent, who was at his best in unrehearsed, improvised "backs to the wall" performances, where his clear beat and faultless stick technique made up for the lack of rehearsal which we so often had to endure during World War Two. Some people maintained wickedly that Sargent deteriorated with every rehearsal, but I do not agree.

My own attempts at conducting were not successful. British orchestras at the time were traditionally against letting anyone conduct them who had not been a professional time-beater all his life. This attitude, I am glad to report, has been relaxed a little in the last few years.

In America, as everyone knows, they have marvellous orchestras almost everywhere, plenty of money is available and consequently, plenty of rehearsing time – never less than two good full-length rehearsals. I remember with the greatest pleasure, working with Mitropoulos and my fellow–Hungarian Eugene Ormandy, alas, now both dead.

Constant Lambert became one of my new great friends and through him I met the Sitwells and William Walton. Alas, death put an end to all these friendships except for Sacheverell Sitwell who is still alive and working. Now, at eighty, I am beginning to feel that it is too late to form new friendships; but an army of young pupils gives me the warmth and affection that everybody needs, at whatever age.

I must, however, mention my dear brother-in-law, Yehudi Menuhin, one of the most valuable human beings it has ever been my good fortune to come across. We became friends even before becoming relations – he married my wife's sister, the dancer Diana Gould – and many public performances and recordings bear witness to the human and artistic affinities that linked us together. It is not often that affectionate brothers-in-law can also be like-minded interpreters of great classical music and I am grateful to be able to say that this happened mainly because of Yehudi's character, which included a flexibility, a willingness to be persuaded (but also a firmness in defending his convictions when put in question) which led to some very good joint performances and a warm personal friendship. In addition to his other qualities, Yehudi has great personal charm, a sense of humour, and a permanent urge of doing, and being, good. His modesty – all the more remarkable in someone who has had perhaps the greatest acclaim of all living artists – is proverbial, and his enthusiasm for other artists, when roused, shines like the unmistakable sign it is of a rare human being.

IX

My involvement with what in the 'Twenties' was termed 'modern' music began, still in Hungary, with performances of works by contemporary composers who were (with the exception of Bartók) all my teachers: Kodály, Bartók, Weiner. It will be obvious that all these composers – again with Bartók as the only exception – wrote 'progressive' music, but music which did not 'progress' beyond the limits of tonality. I was passionately fond of early twentieth-century composers. My repertoire included most of the works of Debussy, Ravel, Scriabine, de Falla, Bloch, Casella etc. Bartók's early piano music fitted into this world very easily. The revolution caused by Schoenberg, first by a totally negative 'atonality', then by the so-called dodecaphonic ('twelve tone') discipline, found me unprepared and unwilling to follow down that road. I thought that the abolition of tonality impoverished music instead of enriching it, and the imposition of a very strict new system, under which all twelve notes of the chromatic scale, in the form of a "tone-row", must be omnipresent throughout the work, did not represent a liberation from the old major-minor scales, but a different kind of slavery – as is often the case with political revolutions. Bartok's case was special. He misunderstood the term 'Twelve Tone' to mean that from now on, with all rules removed, it was the composer's right to use the twelve notes of the chromatic scale as he wished. He tried it, moreover, but luckily his innate musicianship and his life as a concert pianist stopped him writing total nonsense. In fact most of his 'progressive' music, on closer inspection, turns out to be quite tonal. As for Schoenberg, I could never accept him, not even in his Wagner–influenced early works. I just cannot believe in his creative gift. My old friend Weiner used to say that 'understandable' stuff is no proof of a creative faculty, any more than the opposite. That is my view of Mahler: quite understandable but not potent.

If, at a tender age, someone had played to me a piece by, say, Schoenberg or Boulez (I not having heard any music before), and had explained: "This is music. Wouldn't you like to be a musician?", my answer quite certainly would have been: "Not on your life! I'd rather be an engine driver." And this is the way I feel about it today. And so, in my eighty-first year, I have decided that what little time is left to me I will devote to the great music I have worshipped all my life, leaving the rest to the younger generation.

It is true that when I first came to England I accepted the prevalent view that a re-creative artist like myself should not be too limited in his choice of repertoire by personal likes and dislikes; all music written in our age deserves at least a hearing. So it happened that I included many contemporary British composers in my repertoire. I played Bax, Lambert, Walton, Ireland, Tippett (giving the first performances of his *Piano Concerto* in England and America), Rawsthorne and others. Most of this music I did like very much, but where the immediate natural sympathy was lacking, I made myself, by hard and insistant exploration of the composer's personality, arrive at that total understanding which is tantamount to an identification with the composer – an intellectual exercise enabling one to play the work as if written by oneself. I recommend this method to young pianists obliged to play unpalatable music.

Epilogue

What, then, is the music that I stated as having worshipped all my life? Perhaps the simplest definition is that it is the kind of music which comes from the heart and goes to the heart, without distinction as to 'new' or 'old'. The one thing I have learnt in my long life of making sounds on the piano, and which has never been in doubt for me, is: all good music is new, but not vice versa.

When an artist reaches his eightieth year, still alive and working, half the critics decree, without listening to his playing, that his faculties are deteriorating, or have deteriorated, and relegate him to some shelf where he may reminisce on past glories. The other half find that he is "better than ever", again without listening, thus maintaining in effect that it is admirable in itself not to be dead. This has happened to Toscanini, Klemperer and others, and, though humility forbids ranging myself with such illustrious artists, it is happening, *mutatis mutandis*, to me. When I was young, I often heard the view that maturity counts for something if not for everything but now that I am old, only the young count, apparently. It is difficult to be born at the right time. But surely Verdi's last operas, written when he was in his eighties, are not marvellous because the composer was old, but because they are marvellous. It would perhaps help towards balanced judgement in matters artistic if the terms 'old' or 'young' were recognised as irrelevant. But perhaps I make this complaint not without bias now that I am in the 'old' category. I should have made it, and didn't, when I was young.

II A peculiar magic

Ronald Stevenson

An apparation of Paganini: that was the thought that haunted my imagination after hearing my first Kentner concert. It was sometime during the second world war and in the Queen's Hall, Blackburn, Lancashire. He played the *Hungarian Fantasy* of Liszt. He was no mere technician, rather a *pyro*technician. When I recall it, more than 40 years later, the vibrancy of his repeated notes still pulsates in my memory. To my youthful impressionability, his dark hair and sharp profile did indeed suggest Paganini. (Age may smile at youth's fancies, but may it be that the divine intoxication of adolescence affords glimpses of truth that are lost to greybeard sobriety?) I am grateful that the vividness of Kentner's playing, first heard so long ago, burnt itself onto my brain for a lifetime.

I recall, too, his dramatic musical and physical gesture that accompanied the *caesura* at the close of a Lisztian cadenza.

Another early Kentner memory is of an exquisitely songful interpretation of Schubert's little A major Sonata. This, too, is an impression that has remained for nearly half a century. It contrasts with some recitals one hears today, which are forgotten within a week.

As a boy I eagerly bought Kentner's records issued on

the blue Columbia label. These included works seldom played by other pianists, such as the John Field *Nocturne Pastorale* in A major and the Schulz-Evler *Arabesques on the Blue Danube.* I remember reading a review of this last which claimed that there were more notes per minute on that record than on any other available at that time! But that comment seemed of little consequence to me in relation to the melting tone and elegant style.

A conviction of mine, held from youth and confirmed in maturity, is that a musician who performs with Kentner's command of detail and overall structure is most probably a composer. This conjecture was confirmed. But more of that later.

During his early years in Britain his activities were many and varied, displaying a versatility not always conducive to public recognition; for the general public best understands a musician who often appears in one and the same role. An example of this versatility was Kentner's soundtrack recording of Richard Addinsell's *Warsaw Concerto* in the British film *Dangerous Moonlight.* I should guess that Kentner wouldn't particularly want to be reminded of this. For my part, I think Addinsell's score was better than most film music at the time. No less a musician than Percy Grainger published an arrangement of it for two pianos. In any case, this work might well have served to introduce a large public to the Tchaikovsky and Rachmaninov piano concertos.

A kind of cognate activity to that film sound-track performance was the wartime recording Kentner made of Constant Lambert's orchestration of Liszt's *Dante Sonata* in piano concerto form, with Lambert conducting the Sadlers Wells Orchestra; a recording used for the Sadlers Wells Ballet Company's wartime tours.

Years passed. One of my own major activities was

research into Busoni. Hawk-eyed for any references, I occasionally noticed that Kentner was programming a work I have never heard any other pianist play; the Meyerbeer-Liszt-Busoni *Ad nos, ad salutarem undam* . . . a monumental transcription.

In 1958, I was a guest speaker at the first Busoni Festival in Empoli, near Florence. I contacted a number of distinguished musicians living in Britain, saying that if they wished to send a greeting to the Festival, I should be happy to read it out. Sir Adrian Boult, Harriet Cohen, Mark Hambourg and Max Rostal all responded warmly. So did Kentner, saying that he had learnt much from the Busoni editions of Liszt.

About 1965 or 1966, Sir William Walton, who had been most encouraging about my own composition *Passacaglia on DSCH*, contacted Kentner with the request that he get to know my work. It was arranged that I visit Kentner in his Chelsea home – a house of real artistry, full of *objets d'art*. He requested that I play my *Passacaglia* for him. He wanted to hear the whole thing, which takes 80 minutes non-stop. At the end, after congratulating me on the work, he was candid enough to say, "I shall not perform this piece. I am now 60. I know my powers. If I were 40, I'd do it. Have you composed some shorter piano works?" I played him my *Prelude, Fugue & Fantasy on Busoni's Faust*. His comment was again frank:

– I shall not perform that either.
– Why not, may I ask?
– Because it finishes quietly, and Liszt never finished an operatic fantasy quietly.
– Busoni did in his *Carmen Fantasy*.
– I don't play that either.

Kentner knows his public. He is a realist in this respect.

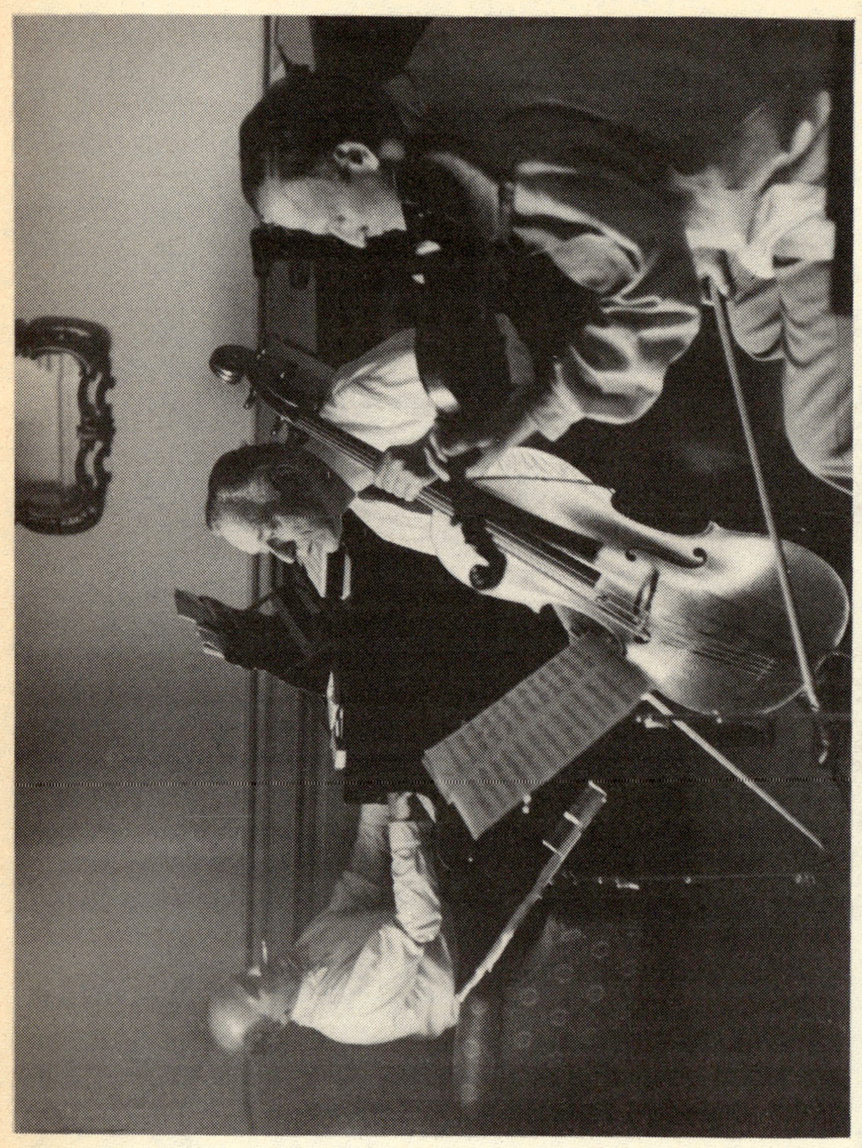

I do not take a superior view of his attitude. It has much in common with Arthur Rubinstein's comment (in his *Memoirs* I think) that the general public still cannot take the whole of Beethoven's *Hammerklavier*.

At that meeting in the Sixties, Kentner requested me to send him a short piano composition of mine, *Little Variations on Purcell's Scotch Tune*, a piece lasting about 5 minutes. He acknowledged receipt, then I heard nothing about it for some nine years. Out of the blue he wrote that he had memorised it and was going to programme it, but he had one request: that I might consider writing one or two new and really brilliant variations, to give variety in contrast to the generally quiet mood of the piece. When I read that request, I threw the letter down, exclaiming: "Virtuoso with itching fingers!" – and muttered blasphemies for a couple of minutes. Then I turned the page of Kentner's letter and read: " . . . but should you think this plan inartistic, I shall play the music as it stands." This made my initially bad-tempered response seem foolish. Disarmed, I wrote two new variations.

Kentner invited me to his home to hear him play my piece. It contains a blues which, at Kentner's hands, sounded like the slow fantasia, the *lassan*, that opens a Hungarian rhapsody. It was certainly a characterful performance. He broadcast it and I was very touched that he programmed it with the Bach-Busoni *Chaconne*, saying to me, "I thought it would please you, as I know you value Busoni."

His programme also included a group of *Bagatelles* by Smetana (including the titles *Innocence* and *Dissonance*). I myself had played these pieces publicly only a short time before, though I'm pretty sure Kentner didn't know that. It was another example of our affinity.

When I first visited Kentner in '65 or '66, he casually

mentioned that he was composing a string quartet. Later I was privileged to peruse the score. In Hungarian chamber music there are three schools: the Germanically-oriented, as exemplified by Dohnányi; the new Hungarian (which in some ways, resurrected the oldest Hungarian folksong), embodied in the work of Bartók and Kodály; and a third school midway between these schools, an exemplar of which was Leo Weiner. Kentner's work belongs to this last genre. Indeed, although I have never discussed it with him, I should guess that Weiner was a salient influence on Kentner's composition generally. This style is characterised by concision, clarity and a rejuvenated classicality, not to be confused with the false Arcady of the 'back to Bach' neo-classicism of the Twenties. Kentner's *Quartet* is in one movement. Its freedom and generosity of line evince the hand of a master-painter of sound, who, to attain such mastery, must have witheld or destroyed more music than he has allowed to remain extant. The *Quartet* ends with the texture being reduced to a single line, which is reminiscent of a procedure in the late music of Liszt.

Already in the late Thirties, soon after his arrival in Britain, Oxford University Press published his three *Sonatinas* for piano. These are not sonatinas in the Clementi sense, meaning small sonatas for children, but, rather, sonatinas in the Busonian sense of fairly extended works in a lyrical and light-textured style, which, while being performable by gifted children, are really works for the concert platform.

Each of these may certainly compare to the Bartók *Sonatina* and, like it, embody Hungarian idioms, particularly the *lassan* (the slow, *parlando* introduction) and the *friska* (the lively Hungarian folkdance).

One of the few works that Kentner has allowed to remain was composed between the *Sonatinas* and the

Quartet. It is the *Divertimento* for chamber orchestra (solo woodwinds, 2 horns, trumpet, timpani, side drum, triangle and strings). The MS is marked: 'Grand Hotel, Dollar, Scotland' and 'Ilkley, Yorkshire, 18–9–41'. There are five movements: March, Nocturne, Scherzino, Intermezzo and Capriccio Finale. The second movement is a *siciliana*. The penultimate movement is a slow *parlando* with solo viola; and the finale is an extended *fugato* on a garrulous and long but joking fugal subject. Considering the increase in the number of chamber orchestras in recent years, this work deserves to receive frequent performance and would enhance and harmonise with a programme that included for instance, Haydn, Mozart or Boccherini.

Recently I bought from a second-hand book dealer a copy of Sacheverell Sitwell's opuscule *La Vie Parisienne*, a charming and perceptive biography of Offenbach. I had read a borrowed copy of the book years ago but had forgotten that it was dedicated to Louis Kentner. This is a most appropriate dedication, for Kentner's aesthetic favours a Latin approach to art, propelled by an Hellenic breeze. This approach united Kentner with his friends Constant Lambert and William Walton. Reconsidering their contribution to the London music scene of the Thirties and Forties, and inevitably contrasting it with the amorphous cultural atmosphere of to-day, we may again experience halcyon delights which, if recaptured in to-day's concerts, would bring new enjoyment and a sorely needed *joie de vivre*.

But thanks be that Kentner continues to give his incomparable recitals, which themselves always recapture something of the refulgence and unalloyed joy of the beauty that was – and *is*! – whenever his fingers wizard the keys into a peculiar magic.

III Forty years on

Harold Taylor

Overhearing a particularly dreary and turgid performance of Brahms' *Paganini Variations* on the radio recently, I was reminded by contrast of the first time I heard Louis Kentner, over forty years ago, when he played this work with such sparkling clarity as to set a standard by which I have found myself judging performances of it ever since. And when I heard him at his eightieth birthday recital, taking the breakneck octaves at the climax of the Liszt *B minor Sonata* in his stride and almost casually reminding us that even *fortissimo prestissimo* textures can be properly balanced and shaped, I was struck by the fact that he had changed so little. Kentner has always worn his virtuosity lightly; "de la musique avant toute chose" might well be the motto of this unostentatious virtuoso.

When Kentner made his New York debut in 1956, this aspect of his art was immediately recognised by the American pianist and composer, Abram Chasins. In his book: *Speaking of Pianists* (Alfred Knopf, New York, 1957), Chasins writes: "He will play the most difficult works with a well-bred effortlessness that conceals the extent of his technical mastery from all but the professional listener. He makes music with a depth and lucidity that place him firmly among the elect of contemporary pianists." This tribue is not quite as glowing as it appears when taken out of its context, for Chasins doesn't place any contemporary pianist at the top of the tree. Chasins was a pupil of the legendary Josef Hofmann, whom he idolised, and much of his book is devoted to the argument that the age of Hofmann, Rachmaninov and their contemporaries was the 'Golden Age' of piano playing, from which there has inevitably been a decline. The conditions under which the performer has to make his way in the modern world, according to Chasins, all conspire towards the elevation of mechanical efficiency above individuality of utterance and depth of understanding.

This is an old cry, as Chasins admits. He says: "Hofmann used to tell me that the emotional intensity and imaginative insight of his leonine master, Anton Rubenstein, made every other pianist sound like a midget", and no doubt Rubenstein said much the same about his idol, Franz Liszt. In some notes on Busoni in my possession, written in 1965, Joseph Szigeti remembers him addressing the Berlin Philharmonic Orchestra at a rehearsal in 1914 with this cryptic remark: "Please, gentlemen – characteristically!" Szigeti explains: "A giant in the history of piano playing, with the most individual and unmistakeable of styles, Busoni was already then reacting against a certain meaningless smooth style of playing which in our time seems to have reached its apex. Quite a few voices have been raised lately about the lack of musical characterisation in our current music making."

By these tokens of continuing decline, 1985 should see us rapidly approaching rock bottom, with the cream of today's virtuosi only distinguished by being less boring than the others, but I suspect that when we cry: "Things aren't what they used to be!", it really means: "We aren't what we used to be." Because we have had so much experience, our boredom threshold is lower, and as new revelations become increasingly difficult to obtain, we tend to invest the heroes of our youth with an aura because they were the ones who gave us our first glimpses of greatness. Nevertheless, it must be admitted that the risk of boredom at current-day piano recitals is greater than it was before the advent of a public nurtured on 'hi-fi' and the long-playing record. 'Thoughtfulness' and 'Textual fidelity' have replaced 'Inspiration' and 'Interpretation' as the important criteria, which is very fortunate for those pianists who have no inspiration to offer, who can convey the letter of a work admirably, but none of its spirit. Most recital programmes are certainly more indigestible than they used to be, often comprising nothing but three or four major works in succession, without any light relief. The great artists may be able to carry off these programmes, but they are often purveyed by a new generation of pianists who approach their task as if they positvely disliked playing the piano in public – a new and disturbing phenomenon.

Although his performance of the *Paganini Variations* lodged in my mind, I did not include Louis Kentner amongst the heroes of my youth. Musically speaking, I was hardly out of short trousers and I have no recollection of how he dealt with the more serious works in a programme which I believe included a Beethoven sonata and the Chopin *'Funeral March' Sonata.* Appreciation of the deeper levels of his art was only to come with the growth of my own musical awareness.

My heroes had already entered Valhalla or were on their way to it. I was an avid collector of gramophone records and also belonged to a generation which still listened to its elders. Tales told of the legendary pianists of pre-war days inspired my collection, and being as prone to self-deception as any other collector, I was quite convinced that those artists whose ghosts I conjured up with the scratch of a needle must *ipso facto* be superior to those I could hear in the flesh. Thus Paderewski, Petri and Rachmaninov stood higher on the slopes of Mount Parnassus than Moiseiwitsch, Solomon or Kentner, with Busoni alone on his Olympian height, a position which he still occupies, although the positions of those on the slopes below have varied considerably over the years. Nowadays the pendulum has swung the other way; youth listens only to youth, and most young musicians appear to be interested only in living performers.

The fact that I was a student at the Royal Manchester College of Music also worked against my fully appreciating Kentner's artistry in those days. In this miniature Leipzig Conservatoire, stolid sobriety was the order of the day and virtuosity was frowned on, unless it was the kind which produced heavyweight performances of the Brahms *Handel Variations*, the *Paganini Variations* being regarded as 'flashy', like the music of Liszt. I was also very much influenced by my first piano teacher at the College, Iso Elinson. Much more a *Brahms–Handel* than a *Brahms–Paganini* player (although he delivered both with equal aplomb) his big round tone and massive legato style were constantly presented to us as an ideal. This was far removed from the leaner athleticism of Kentner, who, in the words of a fellow-student: "made the piano sound like thousands of tiny silver bells" in comparison.

There was another reason why we tended to regard Kentner as a 'lightweight' pianist – he made everything sound so easy. We were taught that making things sound 'too easy' was more of a sin than a virtue, since it could often go against the nature of the music, particularly in Beethoven and Brahms. For example, the downward-leaping octave which begins the *Op.111 Sonata* of Beethoven had to be taken with the left hand only; to divide it between the hands was to weaken the dramatic impact of the music. Nowadays I am more inclined to the view that the easier the player makes his task, the greater should be his possibilities of creating a dramatic impact or any other impression. How difficult it is to listen to a performance objectively! As Kentner has pointed out, an interpretation is no more than the sum of its details. Unfortunately, many details may be missed if the ears of the listener are tuned to a different 'wavelength' than those of the performer, or even if one's feelings about what constitutes the correct gesture are not matched by what one sees happening on the platform.

I cannot pretend to have had a sudden revelation; my conversion to the Kentner cause took place gradually over the years, unlike Abram Chasins, who in a parallel case, suddenly found himself listening with new ears to Josef Lhevinne, as he recounts in *Speaking of Pianists*. Lhevinne died in 1944. After hearing an L.P. re-issue of some of his recordings, some twelve years later, Chasins writes: "I felt an utter fool. At first, I was humiliated to remember that I had once dared to sit in critical judgment of Lhevinne's art and to regard it as incomplete. Then I realised what had happened to me and my standards – how I had unconsciously been seduced and persuaded to yield to contemporary criteria of piano mastery. "This corresponds closely to my feelings about Kentner, except that Chasins is a reluctant convert, as the context makes clear. Still clinging to his 'Golden Age' fantasy, Chasins maintains that he has been won over by Lhevinne, not because his own taste has developed, but because his own standards have unconsciously declined!

Despite his misgivings, Chasins gives the record a 'rave notice', then goes on to express his thankfulness for being able to refer to discs, " . . . . . for in this way the reader and I can share certain sounds that he may not have experienced, sounds that my memory can never erase." This reminds me immediately of a remark by Louis Kentner, taken, like others in this chapter, from conversations with the author: "Josef Lhevinne had a great influence on me; the sound of his playing is something I have carried in my ear all my life."

That statement should not surprise anyone who is familiar with the playing of both artists, if only from gramophone records. Lhevinne was one of the first 'modern' pianists. Disdaining the 'grand manner' of most of his contemporaries, he used his remarkable gifts to present the music with a minimum of distortion and the maximum amount of poetry. Kentner speaks of his "golden tone"; Chasins says: "his sounds glittered and flowed", all of which can be appreciated in some measure from his small legacy of '78' recordings. Amongst these is his marvellous performance of the Schulz–Evler transcription of the *Blue Danube Waltz*. Kentner's own 1940's record of this piece is now also a collector's item, and I was pleased to discover that he was inspired to learn it as a direct result of hearing a performance of it by Lhevinne. As may be expected, both recordings display more similarities than differences. Both artists are forced to make cuts, but Kentner preserves the whole of the introduction – myriads of ethereal silver bells here! – and is not so abrupt in his handling of the transitions between sections. Both recordings exemplify the sheer magic commanded by those few pianists who have complete mastery of rhythm and colour. In the final analysis, these two elements of fine piano playing are inseparable; one can divide the kingdom of the piano between those who can play a Viennese waltz and those who can't.

Another elegant virtuoso who influenced the young Kentner was Emil von Sauer, best known today for his spacious recordings of the Liszt concertos, made in 1939 when he was seventy-seven. Yet though Sauer was a pupil of Liszt, Kentner warns that his editions of Liszt are "not sufficiently respectful" in textual matters. The same may be said of his Chopin editions, although they do not go as far as the notorious Klindworth-Scharwenka edition in 'improving' what Chopin wrote. As Kentner has pointed out: "There is no such thing as an *Urtext*" (if there were, why do so-called *Urtext* editions differ?), but modern editors are at last modest enough to keep their own ideas separate from the composer's text as they perceive it.

Other admired pianists included Moriz Rosenthal, another pupil of Liszt, whose dazzling improvisations on Viennese waltzes are still preserved on disc, and Vladimir de Pachmann, noted for both his beauty of tone and his antics on the concert platform. There has been much speculation as to whether Pachmann was actually mad or simply an eccentric showman. The following experience of Kentner should help to decide: "One of my most cherished memories is of hearing Pachmann in Budapest – a beautiful pianist, but what a charlatan! It was quite a circus when he came on the platform, led by a little boy. First the stool was not high enough, so the boy fetched him a book to sit on, but that made it too high, so he tore off the top page of the book, which made it all right! Then he made comments all the time as the recital progressed, but there was a wonderful spontaneity about the playing and I enjoyed it immensely. The following day, I travelled to Berlin, and the first thing I saw when I arrived was a poster advertising a concert by Pachmann, so of course I had to go and hear this wonderful pianist again. To my great disappointment, the whole performance – the boy, the chair, the book – everything, including the commentary, was repeated in exact detail, the only difference being that in Berlin he spoke German, whereas in Budapest he had spoken in French. The madness had a Method!"

Two pianists who disappointed him were Hofmann and Godowsky. When Kentner heard Hofmann he sounded "curiously pedantic, as if he had chiselled away at his intepretations until only the dry bones were left". As for Godowsky: "He was an absolutely fantastic pianist, who could do things at the piano which none of us could equal – but so austere! I heard him give a wonderful performance of the *Études Symphoniques* of Schumann, which left me completely cold." Corroboration of these opinions comes from Harold C. Schonberg, for many years music critic of the *New York Times*. In his book: *The Great Pianists* (Gollancz, London, 1964), he notes that Hofmann played with greater freedom in the two decades after 1920, judging from a comparison of his early recordings with later 'live' performances of the same pieces which Schonberg heard, and that Godowsky played with much more warmth and spontaneity at private gatherings than in public, a fact also remarked on by Chasins. Schonberg also quotes a review by George Bernard Shaw of an early (1890) performance by Godowsky of the very work mentioned by Kentner, in which Shaw felt that he was inhibited by "a certain shyness, rather engaging than otherwise." It could well be that this shyness hardened into aloofness over the years.

Louis Kentner was not fortunate enough to hear Busoni, but he did hear Rachmaninov, whom he describes as the greatest all-round of all the pianists he has heard, an opinion shared by most of his contemporaries. He voices his high regard for Rachmaninov's Liszt playing in one of the chapters which he wrote for Alan Walker's symposium: *Franz Liszt – the Man and his Music* (Barrie and Jenkins, London, 1970). In this chapter, entitled *The interpretation of Liszt's piano music*, he explains why, in order to be a good Liszt player, one must also be a good player of Beethoven, Mozart, Schubert and Bach, not to mention Debussy and Bartók. Louis Kentner's own ability to grasp the essence of so many different styles has been so well demonstrated in his concerts, that it is a pity that the recording companies have concentrated mainly on his Liszt repertoire, and not devoted an equal amount of needle time to his equally fine interpretations of the *Wanderer Fantasy* of Schubert, or his *Bb major Sonata* or Beethoven's *Les Adieux Sonata* or *op.110*, to name just a few of the works which spring to mind. Perhaps one of the more enterprising record companies will atone for the industry's neglect of his eightieth birthday (also disgracefully ignored by the BBC), by inviting him to record some non-Liszt music for his eightyfifth, or preferably sooner. In this connection, nothing could be more valuable than to have the fruits of his life-long devotion to the '48' available on disc, now that we are beginning to hear Bach played on the piano again after far too long a domination of the musical scene by the cult of 'authenticiy'.

In an imperfect world, we must be grateful for what we have, and especially for Louis Kentner's Mozart recordings, which include a particularly inspired account of the *A major Concerto, K.414*, in partnership with Sir Thomas Beecham. In a typically modest concert-interval talk, broadcast many years ago, Kentner said: "I came late to Mozart, after Beethoven, and even Schumann", and explained how his love of Mozart had intensified through playing concertos with Beecham. He finished by saying: " . . . . but what I can tell you about myself, I can tell you far better in music." These remarks remind me of an essay by Edwin Fischer, in his small but important collection: *Reflections on Music* (Williams and Norgate, 1951), in which he argues that true understanding of Mozart can only come at a late stage in the development of the individual; until then one cannot bring to Mozart what he demands: "An harmonious personality." This performance of *K.414* reveals an undoubtedly harmonious personality at work, which holds all the elements in perfect balance, yet blends without blandness, being at the same time finely tuned to register every little surprise, every nuance of a composer who, as Fischer says: " . . . had more sense impressions, more changes of feeling at one time, than an ordinary man."

Another early recording which deserves special mention, is Debussy's *Children's Corner Suite*. In his book: *Piano* (Macdonald and Jane's, 1976) Kentner describes the work as "enchanting", a word that might stand equally well for his performance of it. Louis Kentner must be one of the few still left alive who heard Debussy play thc piano. This is how he recalls the occasion: "Debussy came to Budapest when I was eight. My parents did not approve of my going to hear him and a lot of other people must have been afraid of being corrupted, because the hall was half empty. To my young eyes he was a frightening figure – a big dark savage with a great black beard. But when he sat down to the piano, he disappeared! At least, that is the impression he gave, he crouched so low over the keys. He accompanied his *Chansons de Bilitis* and played *Children's Corner*. He played so quietly that I had to strain my ears to hear him. When he began *Dr. Gradus ad Parnassum* we hardly knew that he had started!" It is perhaps worth mentioning that the young Kentner was so corrupted by this apostle of degenerate modernity that he included the *Children's Corner Suite* in the programme of his triumphant Berlin début some eight years later.

Art, like life, does not stand still; to my ear, Kentner's playing has grown more passionate over the years, whilst still retaining its sense of proportion and feeling for tonal balance. This trend is observable if one compares the *Lassu* sections of his two L.P. recordings of Liszt's *Second Hungarian Rhapsody*, the first dating from 1954, the second issued in 1971. The latter performances sounds much more dramatic, yet it is only sixteen seconds shorter than the first, which sounds positively elegaic by comparison. There is also a greater feeling of continuity nowadays, a more seamless knitting together of the elements of the larger forms. Listening to one of his recent performances of the *F minor Ballade* of Chopin, I was struck by the way in which the performance flowed from beginning to end, whereas in his recording of twenty years ago, it seems to be presented more as a series of "golden moments".

This ability to sustain a musical line has always been present, if less developed, as witness his 1939 recording of *La Leggierezza*. Here, resisting the temptation to dazzle or thunder, or engage in any other indulgence, Kentner subsumes virtuosity into poetry in a continuous stream of lyricism unmatched by any other performance I know. In the same year he recorded *La Bénédiction de Dieu dans la solitude* and even earlier, Liszt's *Ballade in B minor*, two works which were great novelties for those days and are still not as widely known as they should be, despite Kentner's persistent and persuasive advocacy. If he has identified himself with these and similar works which demand the utmost in lyrical expressiveness which the piano can offer, that is how it should be, because the ability to make the piano 'sing' is the highest form of pianistic art.

The creation of the illusion of 'singing tone' involves nearly everything to do with playing the piano: rhythm, touch, phrasing, pedalling, finger independence, 'voicing' and 'orchestration', and so on, but above all, the pianist's ears. Whatever the state of the player's physical co-ordination, the results he obtains in performance are determined entirely by the extent of his aural imagination and the quality of his aural discrimination. Fine performances are the product of fine-tuned ears, and the greatest artists are the greatest listeners.

It need hardly be said that Louis Kentner has an exceptionally well-tuned pair of ears, as his pupils soon discover. Another facet of his aural virtuosity is his ability to sense the underlying harmonic structure of even the sparest textures, so that what might be rattled through in lesser hands as mere 'passage work' is given shape and purpose. A colleague of mine neatly described this interpretive strength as the capacity to 'explain' the music. It is perhaps no accident that so many of the best interpreters, the ones who really 'explain' the music, are, like Kentner, composers, or have studied composition, which is the most fruitful way of developing one's capacity for 'inner hearing'.

We must be grateful that teaching has played a large part in Louis Kentner's scheme of things for the past forty years or more; all the more so because his teaching operates on the same high level as his playing. He has expressed his philosophy of teaching in *Piano*: " . . . . . no teacher can put anything into a pupil which is not already there. He can only awake what is already lying dormant, and guide it towards possible short cuts, tending and nurturing it as it grows." The gardening metaphor is very apt; taking it further, we could say that he neither attempts to force unnatural growth ("Bring the *Hammerclavier* and six Chopin studies to next week's lesson"), nor retard growth by drastic pruning ("Your technique is impossible; we must spend the next six months on finger exercises"). Kentner accepts what the pupil brings and builds on it, teaching only music and its interpretation. Technical suggestions are offered only as the need arises, for the solution of purely musical problems. As one student put it: "He does not disturb", but leads the pupil gradually out of the cramped world of the 'technical method' towards that world of freedom where the tone-making gestures flow unimpeded in immediate response to the musical image.

All of Louis Kentner's pupils who have written elsewhere in this book have remarked on the high standards which he expects, but he demands no less from himself. Climbing the last flight of stairs to his third-floor studio one morning, I was stopped in my tracks by the sounds of Liszt's *Weinen, Klagen Variations* which leapt at me through the half-open door. I sat on the stairs to listen, realising that this was no 'run through' for the sake of 'keeping the work in the fingers' (phrases which tell their own sorry story), but a concert performance of searing intensity and passion, the final chorale singing its way to heaven with all the resources at the artist's command engaged. Schumann advised young musicians to play always as if a master were listening; here in his turn, a great master was communing with the gods. It has been a privilege and an education to have been able to overhear Louis Kentner during this last forty years, whether on the concert platform or elsewhere. Let us hope we are given the opportunity for many more years to come.

IV The artist as teacher

SIMON NICHOLLS:

As a pianist and a human being Louis Kentner is a romantic and an aristocrat. Associated by the general public, perhaps, with Liszt and Chopin, he brings a full-blooded, living commitment to an enormous repertoire from Bach to Bartók. Perhaps his greatest asset as a teacher is this breadth and depth of knowledge combined with a faculty of total and instant recall which enables him to play immediately from memory any work of the standard repertoire (and many outside it!) which a student cares to bring to him, so that one is presented directly with his own vivid conception.

Elements of his playing which inspire emulation are its absolute relaxation (rarely can the cycle of Chopin's *op. 25 Etudes* have been played with so little apparent effort as at a recital I attended), an easy tone production, quite without hardness yet able to fill the largest of halls, the ability unmistakeably to characterise a work from the first note to the last and an extremely wide tonal palette – this last being allied to a highly developed pedal technique. A refined tonal balance within textures enables him to use the sustaining pedal for long stretches in a way which would bring many lesser mortals to grief. Neither is the third pedal, accidental contact with which most of us spend our pianistic lives trying to avoid, neglected – listen to the beautiful effect it creates at the end of *La Leggierezza*.

Fingering is equally individual. Like Bartók, he is fond of taking successions of single or double notes with the same finger or fingers – or, as he puts it, "a bunch of fingers". The tremolando at the climax of Ravel's *Jeux d'eau* is played with both fists, creating a *fff* of great power. Chords are sometimes played in an unusual position with the thumb under the hand. His muscular freedom enables him to take all repetitions without changes of finger.

At the Menuhin School we were privileged a couple of years back to hear the complete Beethoven sonata cycle from Louis Kentner. His Beethoven is utterly romantic in conception, with the freedom and spontaneity of spoken declamation. In this respect it is quite unlike most of the Beethoven playing to be heard today; perhaps the closest parallel might be with that of Frederic Lamond, some of whose Beethoven interpretations survive on record and who, as is well known, studied with Liszt.* Particularly vivid in my own mind are the revelatory wit and elegance of *op.31 no. 1*, a volcanic, towering *Appassionata*, a glowing *op.109* and an *op.110* of magisterial and Olympian spaciousness. But I shall remember equally the irresistable, smiling charm of *op.49 no. 2*.

There have been opportunities at the School over the last few years for many pupils to play violin, viola and 'cello sonatas with Louis Kentner, and the School Orchestra, conducted by the School's music director, Peter Norris, has collaborated with him in concertos. Each occa-

* Kentner has no recollection of hearing Lamond. – Ed.

sion, whether rehearsal or public performance, has been memorable for the atmosphere of enjoyment and spontaneity together with music-making of great intensity.

Those who attend Louis Kentner's classes can also expect to hear reminiscences of Debussy, Prokofiev, Richard Strauss, Kodály, Bartók and many others, told with the precision and vividness of a born raconteur. This is just one more facet of an extraordinarily rich musical personality.

JULIAN JACOBSON:

I became a pupil of Louis Kentner in 1972, a year after I had come down from Oxford. Oxford had been a wonderful experience and had done much to encourage me to perform, but it was a small and friendly society with no strong instrumental tradition and it was easy to forget the relentlessly high standards that I was going to have to achieve and maintain in order to become a professional pianist.

From my first lesson with Louis I was swept into a world where those standards were constantly held before me. In that wonderful, serene studio of his, I breathed an ineffably noble atmosphere, one that spoke of both the high seriousness and the charm of the pianist's calling – in fact, of the true meaning of the word 'virtuoso'. All this was so different from my own world of rented rooms, piano teaching to little boys in order to pay the rent, auditions, bits and pieces of accompanying and squashed-in practice sessions, that I looked forward to my fortnightly lesson as an oasis of calm and considered work. Louis did not teach me technique as such; I did no exercises with him. There was no overt 'method' and he spoke little of fingers, wrists or arms. Yet within my first two lessons, by a few almost casual remarks aided by a few gentle nudgings and proddings of my arms and shoulders, he succeeded in transforming my technique for life. In non-technical terms I would say that he made me aware that the fundamental act of touch was something infinitely freer, more generous, subtle and varied than I had been using. I knew instantly that this was the direction in which I had to go; I also knew that it would take me a long time to get there, since it involved the relinquishment of a way of playing in which I had at least been able to 'get by', and slowly developing a completely new set of physical feelings. At the beginning, I felt as if I had no control and that I would never be able to play anything difficult again. Fortunately I was free of concert engagements at that time, so I was able to spend hours playing the simplest things imaginable, such as five-finger exercises and pieces from the Schumann *Album for the Young*, in order slowly to gain a new freedom and control.

As in the technical aspect, so in the musical; the single word I would use to describe Louis' teaching is: 'freedom'. Nothing was allowed to be played literally or taken for granted; everything had to be shaped, coloured, made to speak. Melodic lines and significant inner voices had to be brought out to a degree which I occasionally thought excessive, at that time; yet Louis – a direct link with the great figures of the past, when much of the music we play was actually contemporary – spoke with the wisdom and experience of a lifetime's concert-giving on the grand scale, so I willingly trusted his ears rather than my own. Now of course, I see that he was right.

Those precious lessons, (all too few, alas, for personal reasons) gave me enough inspiration for a lifetime's playing. Thank you Louis; and may I wish you many more happy years of playing and teaching.

PHILIP MARTIN:

As a teacher, Louis Kentner sets extremely high standards and will never settle for anything less than the complete observation of every detail in a score. I found his teaching most helpful in the Romantic literature, but also extremely interesting in contemporary music. (We should not forget that he has given the first performances of concertos by Bartók, Tippett and Rawsthorne, amongst many other works.)

I returned several times with the same work (the Tchaikovsky Concerto no.1, for example) and was never disappointed. Louis was always coming up with fresh ideas. His own playing has a wonderful freshness and originality about it. As a composer himself, he is re-creating while he plays, rather than just spinning notes. He belongs to the old romantic school which today is slightly out of fashion. He used to say occasionally: "No wrong notes allowed! Only old men like me can get away with playing a few from time to time", but he plays incredibly few of them, anyway!

I studied with him on and off from 1971 to 1980. I am one of his greatest fans and I feel I owe such a lot to him that I will never be able to repay. I never play a note without thinking of him. It sounds like hero-worship, but that is how I feel.

MARGUERITA WOLFF:

When, as a very young girl I went to play to Louis Kentner he told me that I played with all the confidence of the experienced concert pianist but not with the thousand and one ways of playing the piano that goes into the making of a concert pianist. Since that day, over many years I have travelled on the marvellous voyage of discovery of playing the piano with Louis Kentner.

I will never forget my first lesson with Kentner. I felt as if a cloudy mirror was dusted to enable me to look inside. The sense of revelation I felt then I still feel every time I go for a lesson.

Louis Kentner is much more than a legendary pianist, a big virtuoso, he is a consumate musician and because of this a very great teacher. He is extraordinarily articulate and has a very literary approach and the gift of word imagery in his teaching.

To study the piano with Kentner is a very total thing. No teaching harmony and counterpoint as one subject and piano as another but an awareness all the time of what the music is doing and where it is going, weaving through different keys.

My sister Dorothy was studying the Liszt *Sonata in B minor* with Kentner. He asked her at one point to say what key the work had arrived at, she could not answer immediately so she had to analyse every harmony and modulation in the work, and he corrected it.

After studying a work with Kentner every phrase has been worked at in meticulous detail. He sets enormous store on tonal balance, not only on the singing line but the balance of a triad. He has such a fine ear that a note missing from a chord, however dense, he immediately hears.

Studying a major work with Kentner is a great experience, his wonderful sense of line and structure knitting the entire work together. He always stresses that when it is all studied and enormously worked at none of the seams must show and the playing must appear so spontaneous that it sounds as if the pianist is composing it at that moment.

Studying a concerto is of course very exciting. He expects you to know the full score, to know the orchestral as well as the solo part. When playing chamber music the same applies and he likes the entire ensemble – duo, trio, quartet etc., to go to his studio.

Once, playing the Cesar Franck *Piano Quintet* with a well known quartet, he suggested some ways of bowing to the string players and also corrected some of their notations. The quartet were so impressed they asked him to coach them with a Haydn string quartet.

Kentner has a huge repertoire. I once asked him if there was anything he did not play, he modestly said "Yes, some works before Bach and some moderns". This for a pupil is colossal. Anything one takes to him he knows and immediately gives a masterly lesson.

I consider myself very privileged and fortunate in learning the 'thousand and one things that go to make a concert pianist' from that very great man, Kentner.

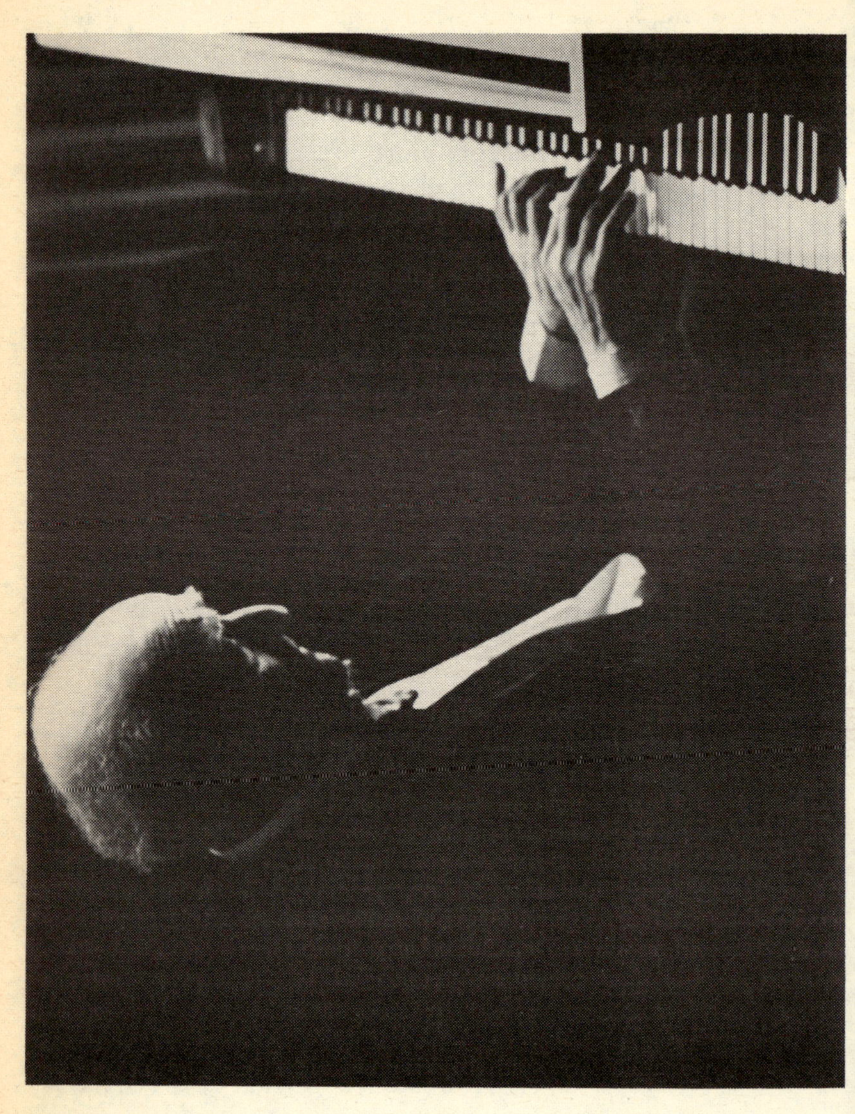

V Tributes

FROM THE LISZT SOCIETY

Mr. Louis Kentner is one of the few professional musicians who, in the first half of this century, was able to perceive the enduring value of much of Liszt's vast musical output. He has always been an untiring champion of his famous compatriot.

Mr. Kentner joined the first Committee of the Liszt Society at its formation in 1951. The rest of the Committee at that time consisted of Professor Edward J. Dent, Ralph Hill, Constant Lambert, the Hon. Edward Sackville-West, Sacheverell Sitwell, Sir William Walton and Humphrey Searle. In 1965 he became the Society's President.

Mr. Kentner has always been a working President, never a mere figurehead, and we owe him much: He has attended many of the Council meetings and taken an active part in the deliberations. His great knowledge and experience of matters musical have been at the Council's disposal whenever needed. What I gratefully remember most of all are the piano recitals he has given for a number of years on the occasion of the Society's Annual General Meeting in the elegant home of Miss Marguerite Wolff. At these meetings we have heard Liszt's piano music played by a master musician in ideal surroundings.

Those privileged to know Mr. Kentner find in him not only a great artist, but also a kindly and well-balanced man with a considerable sense of humour. His repertoire of anecdotes has enlivened many a dull business session.

For all the work he has done for music we can but say: "Thank you!"

Vernon Harrison Ph.D.
Chairman: *The Liszt Society*

Amongst many activities generously undertaken for the Liszt Society, Louis Kentner was Chairman of the jury at the British Liszt Piano Competition held in September 1976 at the University of Surrey, when first prize in the senior section was awarded to Terence Judd. Earlier in the same year, he gave a series of four master classes on two consecutive weekends in the small concert room at 268 Brompton Road (now sadly closed).

In March 1983 a more ambitious series of master classes was held at the Purcell Room, culminating in a Queen Elizabeth Hall recital which included all six pupils taking part in a performance of Liszt's *Hexameron* with one variation being taken by each pupil in turn. The Purcell Room classes took place on three consecutive afternoons. Thanks are due to the anonymous donor who gave financial support to this prestigious series.

Louis Kentner has played almost every year at the Society's Annual General Meetings held at the home of Miss Marguerite Wolff, where he also gave a programme of twentieth century Hungarian music in March 1979 when we were joined by members of the British – Hungarian Fellowship. A highlight of the Hungarian Liszt Society's trip to Britain in July 1981 was the Gala Evening organised jointly by ourselves and the European Piano Teachers Association, when Mr. Kentner played the complete *Années de Pèlerinage* Book 2 and was presented with a plaque by Professor Miklós Forrai. Nor shall we forget his splendid recital in Norwich in March 1984, held under the auspices of the Liszt Society and organised by one of our members. This took place in the Georgian Assembly Rooms where Liszt himself had played in 1838 and Mr. Kentner's programme included the rarely heard *Grand Solo de Concert*.

Alan Paul
Activities Organiser: *The Liszt Society*

FROM THE CHOPIN SOCIETY

In appreciation of our President, Louis Kentner, I would like to say a few words about this remarkable musician. At the age of eighty, he plays with all the fire and poetry of a much younger man. He is a splendid teacher, and many young musicians have cause to be grateful to him for his inspiration and dedication. Mr. Kentner is an authority on Liszt and few pianists, if any, can surpass him in his interpretation of that composer's piano works.

We are indeed fortunate that Mr. Kentner graciously consents to play for our Society from time to time and we wish him health and strength to continue his work as a teacher and concert pianist. Our Society is all the richer for having Louis Kentner as our President.

Lucie Swiatek
Founder–Organiser: *The Chopin Society*
(founded 1971 in London)

FROM THE EUROPEAN PIANO TEACHERS ASSOCIATION

On his eightieth birthday, EPTA (UK) salutes Louis Kentner, its President, friend and supporter, the supreme artist who has given his generous assistance on so many occasions.

At the launching of EPTA in March 1978, he took part in the celebrations and gave an unforgettable recital. In 1980, we paid tribute to Louis Kentner on his seventy-fifth birthday when he joined pianists and piano teachers from many parts of the world at the European Conference of EPTA Associations at Royal Holloway College. To thank the distinguished audience, he sat at the piano and gave superlative performances of Beethoven's op.109 and Chopin's *Sonata in B minor.*

His most memorable appearance was at the Gala Evening organised jointly by EPTA and the Liszt Society in 1981 at the Guildhall School of Music and Drama, in honour of the Hungarian Liszt Society's visit to England. His recital was entirely devoted to Liszt's music, and the evening ended with the President of the Hungarian Liszt Society presenting Mr. Kentner with a plaque making him an honorary member of the Society. It was a most moving occasion and he was greeted by Hungarian friends whom he had not seen for many years.

In 1984, Louis Kentner gave a fine recital in Hastings on the occasion of the launching of EPTA there, and in 1986 he will preside over the jury at the International Piano Competition organised by EPTA NEDERLAND to commemorate the centenary of Liszt's death.

EPTA wishes Louis Kentner many more years of artistic achievements.

Carola Grindea
Founder and Organising Secretary: *EPTA*

Dear Mr Taylor,

I was delighted to hear that you are producing a volume of tributes to Louis Kentner, and I don't want to miss this opportunity of adding my tribute to him on his 80th Birthday.

It is hard to think that he has reached this magic age. He has such vitality and youthfulness of spirit, both in his attitude to life and in his music-making. But I have to believe the evident fact that he *is* eighty, and join in the birthday greetings and expressions of admiration and affection.

Like many others, I have two causes for gratitude to Louis, one as a music lover and listener, the other as a pupil. My listening days go back to the war-time National Gallery concerts in which Louis Kentner was a frequent and much-loved performer. He had come to this country in 1935, just fifty years ago, and in these five decades has enriched our musical life wonderfully. He is one of that band of musical refugees who chose this country, to the lasting benefit of our cultural life. Britain can be proud to have opened its doors to many outstanding artists and, above all, grateful for what it gained as a result. Thus Louis Kentner has brought immeasurable happiness to generations of music lovers here, as well as abroad. How lucky for us that he chose England as his home.

Others can explain better than I the particular magic of his pianism. He is one of the survivors of that great tradition of romantic pianists and every aspiring young pianist ought to hear him play. Not for him the emphasis on fireworks or show-off techniques. True, his technique is formidable, but it is always subservient to the music. Anyone who heard him play the Liszt *B Minor Sonata* at his Queen Elizabeth Hall Birthday Concert will know what I mean. Many pianists can play that work with bravura brilliance, making it sound almost as a series of Czerny exercises. But few can bring out, as Kentner does, the poetry and romanticism as well as the brilliance. The same is true of all his playing. Invariably, it is marked by total musical integrity and faithfulness to the composer's intention, and a lovely serenity and sensitivity. In fact, he brings to his playing a rare combination of the head, the heart and the fingers – with a memory and accuracy send almost to none.

All this has brought, and continues to bring, happiness to hundreds of thousands of listeners over the years. A smaller band – his pupils – have an even deeper cause for gratitude. To me this privilege came late in life – just under 4 years ago – and, since I am an amateur pianist rather than a professional, I am in a particular category. But I benefit just a much from his greatness as a teacher. In fact, I doubt whether there have been, or are, many teachers to equal his gifts. Lessons are of course tough and praise is rare – which I am sure is right. Perfectionism in accuracy and technique is a constant aim, but above all there is his emphasis on the music and the composer's intention. One is taught a great deal about music, about art in general and, in a real sense, about life. Lessons are not dry instructions of how to play a piece, more a revelation of what it is all about, what one is trying to express or experience through the music – for one's own benefit and for anyone who might be listening.

Louis Kentner has an uncommonly good ear, and no inaccuracy will escape him, nor the slightest variant from desirable pedalling. Many remarks remain in my memory, often coupled with a good dose of Hungarian humour (his fund of musical anecdotes is unrivalled) – here is a small sample:

"I think we had better clean up that bar."

"Why play the wrong note when the right one is right next door."

"Yes, of course you can occasionally play the wrong note once I am convinced you actually hear it."

"The right note is no harder to play than the wrong one."

"Has the left hand been on holiday?"

"I think a drop of pedal would help here."

"The way you start that piece should be much more timid. You play it with a strength and confidence suggesting that you know what is to come, whereas in fact it ought to sound as if you don't."

"Move your arms around more. They should live above the keyboard, not on it."

"I think you should use all the fingers democratically."

And so on. Many comments on the music are of great subtlety, steeped in years of committed musicianship. I come away from each lesson worn out by the necessary concentration, but inspired by the sensitivity, wide learning and musicianship Louis Kentner brings to his lessons. I am sure that all his pupils feel the same and, whatever their level of performance, are immensely enriched by all that Louis brings into their lives.

So, on this occasion, I salute a fine musician, a great teacher and a most lovable human being; and my salute also – of course – encompasses his lovely Griselda, who is so totally part of Louis' life and music.

Claus Moser, 7th August 1985

Kentner

Dear Harold Taylor,

I find it very difficult to believe that *Louis Kentner* is going to have his 80th birthday in July – perhaps that is because *I am seven years older than him!* The two *most wonderful and inspiring musical memories of my own lifetime* are his performances of *Liszt* and the equalling – but so different – performances of *Mrs. Gordon Woodhouse* on her clavichord. Ah! Well! it is wonderful to have been alive and to have had these magical experiences of music.

Yours sincerely,
Sacheverell Sitwell
6th March 1985

Discography

Only recordings issued in Great Britain are listed; many of them are also to be found in foreign catalogues under different labels, but these catalogues do not appear to contain any additional material. In the '78' section, where two numberings are given for the same recording, the second indicates 'automatic' couplings, i.e. the sides are paired non-sequentially for use with the automatic record-changing mechanisms of the period.

78 RPM RECORDINGS

Edison Bell *12″ (1928)*

NUMBER	COMPOSER	TITLE
DX 543	Chopin	Impromptu no. 1 in A flat
		'Fantaisie-Impromptu' in C sharp minor

(For an interesting review of this rare disc, see James Methuen-Campbell: *Chopin Playing*; Gollanz 1981)

Columbia (1937–1950) 12″ Dark Blue (DX), 10″ Dark Blue (DB) or 12″ Light Blue (LX)

NUMBER	COMPOSER	TITLE
DX 777	Liszt	Hungarian Rhapsody no. 2
DX 784	″	Au Bord d'une Source
		Feux Follets
DX 851–2	″	Ballade no. 2 in B minor
DX 864–5	″	Venezia e Napoli
DX 879–80	″	Bénédiction de Dieu dans la solitude
DX 895–6	Chopin	Andante Spianato et Grande Polonaise Brillante
DX 908	Mozart	Rondo in D, K 485
	Liszt	Waldesrauschen

DX 912–916	Beethoven	Sonata in B flat op. 106
DX 8139–8143		('Hammerklavier')
DX 923	Meyerbeer-Liszt	Scherzo ('Les Patineurs')
LX 759–61	Beethoven	Violin Sonata in F, op. 23
LX 8406–9408		('Spring') with Jeno Léner (violin)
LX 827–9	"	Violin Sonata in A, op. 30 no.
LX 8449–8451		1 with Jeno Léner (violin)
DX 943	Schubert-Liszt	Soirée de Vienne no. 6
DX 946	Delibes-Dohnanyi	'Naila' Waltz
DX 960	Liszt	Concert Study in F minor ('La Leggierezza')
		Concert Study in D flat ('Un Sospiro')
DB 1903	Schumann	Arabeske
DX 967–8	Liszt orch. Lambert	'Dante' Sonata with Sadlers Wells Orchestra conducted by Constant Lambert
DX 972–3	Bartók	Duets for Children
	Walton	Popular Song ('Facade') with Ilona Kabos
DX 986	Liszt	Polonaise no. 1 in C minor
DX 987	"	Hungarian Rhapsody no. 9 ('Carnaval de Pesth')
DX 988–9	Liszt	Scherzo and March
	Bartók	Children's Pieces nos. 22, 23, 32, 42. (Bk. 4)
DX 997	Chopin	Fantasy-Impromptu
		Impromptu in F sharp
DX 1006	Liszt	Berceuse
LX 894–6	Mozart	Concerto in A major K 414 with
LX 8489–8491		London Philharmonic Orchestra cond. Sir Thomas Beecham
DX 998–100	"	Trio in E flat K 498 with Reginald Kell (clarinet) & Frederick Riddle (viola)

DX 1007–9	Brahms	Trio in A minor op. 114 with Kell & Riddle
DX 1038	Liszt	Liebestraume no. 3
		Gnomenreigen
DX 1081	Chopin	Impromptu in A flat
		Waltz in C sharp minor op. 64 no. 2
DX 1017	Dvorak	Trio in E minor op. 90 ('Dumky') with Henry Holst (violin) and Anthony Pini ('cello)
DX 1062	Addinsell	'Warsaw' Concerto with London Symphony Orchestra cond. Richard Addinsell
DX 1083	Chopin	Study in C minor op. 10 no. 12 ('Revolutionary')
		Polonaise in A
DX 1093	Schubert	Impromptu in A flat op. 90 no. 4
DB 2100	Paganini-Liszt	Study in E flat
DX 1121	Debussy	'Children's Corner' nos. 1–4
		'Children's Corner' nos. 5–6
	Schumann	Träumerei
DX 1129	John Field	Nocturne in G major
		Nocturne in A major
DX 1146–7	Chopin	Polonaise-Fantaisie op. 61
		Nocturne in B op. 32 no. 1
DX 1175	Balakirev	Islamey
DX 1184	Strauss–Schulz-Evler	'Blue Danube' Concert Paraphrase
DX 1237	Balakirev	Rêverie
		Mazurka no. 6 in A flat
DX 1391	Chopin	Ballade in G minor op. 23
DX 1502	"	Polonaise in A flat op. 53
DX 1543–1545 DX 8325–7	Beethoven	Sonata in F minor op. 57 ('Apassionata')
DX 1580	Paganini-Liszt	'La Campanella'
		'La Chasse'
DX 1626	Chopin	Scherzo in E op. 54
DX 1640	"	Bolero op. 19

Kentner

DX 1760–2	Liszt	Sonata in B minor
DX 8385–8386		
DX 1775	Beethoven	Für Elise
		Bagatelle in A minor (Grove 173)
		Rondo in B flat (British Museum mss.)
DX 1813	Liszt	Csardas Macabre
DX 1822	"	En rêve
		Richard Wagner – Venezia
DX 1859	Chopin	Scherzo in B minor op. 20
LX 1407–9	Balakirev	Sonata in B flat minor
LX 8810–12		
LX 1428–36	Liapounov	Twelve Transcendental Studies op. 11

LONG PLAYING RECORDINGS (1954–1975)

With a few indicated exceptions, these are all 12″, 33 rpm. 7″ 45 rpm 'extended-play' records have lower case prefixes. The *Columbia* and *Saga* recordings are all monophonic; in other cases, the presence of the letter 'S' in a prefix or suffix indicates a stereophonic disc.

Columbia

33SX 1014	Liszt	Hungerian Rhapsodies no. 2, 6, 12, 15.
33SX 1033	Chopin	The Four Scherzos
sed 5519	Liszt	Csardas Macabre, En Rêve, Richard Wagner-Venezia

Saga

XID 5238	Beethoven	Sonata in B flat op. 106 ('Hammerklavier')
XID 5233	Chopin	The Four Ballades
		Barcarolle op. 60

HMV–EMI

ALP 1565	Beethoven	Andante Favori in F
	Chopin	Impromptu in A flat
		Nocturne in D flat
		Fantasy Impromptu

	Gounod-Liszt	'Faust' waltz
	Liszt	Petrach Sonnets nos. 47, 104, 103
ALP 1050	Beethoven	Violin Sonatas nos. 1 – 3
ALP 1105	"	Violin Sonatas nos. 5 & 10
ALP 1338	"	Violin Sonatas nos. 4 & 2
ALP 1354	"	Violin Sonatas nos. 6 & 7
ALP 1376	"	Violin Sonatas nos. 8 & 9 with Yehudi Menuhin (violin)
ALP 1547	Mozart	Violin Sonatas in A (K526) & B flat (K454) with Yehudi Menuhin (violin)
BLP (10") 1026	Bach	Violin Sonatas 1 and 2 with Yehudi Menuhin
BLP 1082	Franck	Violin Sonata with Yehudi Menuhin (violin)
ALP 1285	Chausson	Concerto in D op. 21 with the Pascal String Quartet
ALP 1621	Beethoven	Sonata in C op. 53 ('Waldstein') Sonata in F minor op. 57 ('Apassionata')
ALP 1704	Brahms	Concerto no. 2 in B flat
ASD 268		Concerto with Philhamonic Orch. cond. Sir Adrian Boult
XLP 20035	Mozart	Concert in C minor K 491 with Philhamonic Orch. cond. Harry Blech
SXLP 20035	"	Sonata no. 17 in D K576
7ep 7110	Chopin	Studies op. 10 nos. 3, 4, 5, 7, 12.
7ep 7115	"	Studies op. 25 nos. 1, 2, 3, 8, 9, 11.
ALP 1849	Ravel	Piano Trio in A minor with Yehudi Menuhin (violin) and Gaspar Cassado ('cello)
ASD 423		

Kentner

ALP 1987	Liszt	*Années de Pèlerinage en Italie:* Sposalizio Il penserioso Canzonetta del Salvator Rosa Fantasia après une lecture de Dante Jeux d'eau a la Ville d'Este Godoliera e Tarantella (Venezia e Napoli)
ALP 1906	Brahms	Violin Sonatas nos. 1 & 2 with Yehudi Menuhin
ALP 1907	Brahms	Violin Sonata no. 3
ASD 475	Schubert	Fantasy for Violin and Piano D934 with Yehudi Menuhin
ASD 4039	Brahms	Violin Sonatas nos. 1& 2 with Yehudi Menuhin

Qualiton

SHLX 90027	Mozart	Rondo alla Turca (from Sonata no. 11)
	Beethoven	Für Elise
	Schubert	Moment Musical no. 3
	Schumann	Träumerei
	Chopin	Two Waltzes, Prelude, Three Studies
	Liszt	Spinning Chorus from Wagner's 'Flying Dutchman' Gnomenreigen Waldesrauschen La Campanella

Vox-Decca Turnabout

TV 34140S TV 4140	Schubert	Piano Quintet ("The Trout") with members of the Hungarian Quartet and Georg Hortnagel (double bass)

TV 34163S TV 4163	Liszt	*Operatic and Dramatic Fantasies:* Reminiscences de 'Don Juan' Spinning Song from Wagner's 'Flying Dutchman' Wedding March and Dance of the Elves from Mendelssohn's 'Midsummer Night's Dream' Music Waltz from Gounod's 'Faust'
TV 34224–5S	Liszt	Transcendental Studies (complete) Ballade no. 2 in B minor Elegy no. 2 Nuages gris La lugubre Gondola
TV 34266–8DS	Liszt	Hungarian Rhapsodies nos. 1–19 (complete)
TV 34310S	Liszt	Harmonies poétiques et religieuses (1834) Four little piano pieces Valse a capriccio sur deux motifs de Lucia et Parisina En Rêve Bénédiction de Dieu dans la solutide Five Hungarian Folk Songs Apparitions no. 1
TV 34444S	Liszt	Spanish Rhapsody Rumanian Rhapsody Concerto Pathétique for Two Pianos with June Havill

Notes on the contributors

Julian Jacobson was born in 1947 and studied at the Royal College of Music and Queen's College, Oxford. He made his London debút in 1974; his career so far includes tours of Europe, the Soviet Union and the USA, and appearances at the major British festivals. A founder-member of the ensemble, *Capricorn*, he is active as a duo and ensemble pianist and has a strong commitment to music of the present time, being also a composer. He has written piano and chamber works, also the score for the TV film of *To the Lighthouse*. Julian Jacobson made his Royal Festival Hall concerto debút in February 1986.

Philip Martin comes frm Dublin. He made his concerto debút at both the Royal Festival and Royal Albert Halls in 1977 and his repertoire in this field contains over forty works. He is also a prolific composer (published by Boosey and Hawkes) and his long-standing interest in American music has gained him a joint UK – USA scholarship for research into American composers. He made his New York début in 1983 and has already made another tour of the United States with his wife, the soprano Penelope Price-Jones, with whom he has a duo partnership. Philip Martin teaches piano at the Birmingham School of Music.

Yehudi Menuhin, the distinguished violinist and conductor, began his career in San Francisco in 1923 at the age of seven and quickly achieved world-wide recognition following his debút with the Berlin Philharmonic Orchestra at the age of twelve. Since the Second World War, he has been a tireless campaigner for international reconciliation and greater understanding between peoples of different creeds and cultures. He was elected President of the International Music Council in 1969 and holds the Nehru Award for International Understanding amongst many world-wide honours.

Yehudi Menuhin founded the Gstaad Festival in 1957; he was also Artistic Director to the Bath Festival (1959–68) and to the Windsor Festival (1969–72). In 1963, he founded the Yehudi Menuhin School for musically-gifted children at Stoke d'Abernon, Surrey – the first of its kind in England – and in 1977 he established *Live Music Now*, which provides a platform for young musicians and seeks audiences outside the traditional venues. His publications include his autobiography: *Unfinished Journey* (1977); *The King, the Cat and the Fiddle*, for younger readers (1983), and the *Menuhin Music Guides* series, of which is is General Editor. Yehudi Menuhin is an honorary Knight Commander of the Order of the British Empire and an honorary Swiss Citizen.

Sir Claus Moser, K.C.B. was born in Berlin in 1922 and is a graduate of the London School of Economics, whose teaching staff he joined in 1946, becoming Professor of Social Statistics from 1961 until 1970. He was Head of the Government Statistical Service from 1967 until 1978 and is now Warden of Wadham College, Oxford. Sir Claus has been Chairman of the Royal Opera House, Covent Garden, since 1974 and has served on the governing bodies of many other scientific and cultural institutions including the Royal Academy of Music, of which he is an honorary Fellow. His published work includes *Measurement of Levels of Living* (1957) and *British Towns* (1961).

Simon Nicholls is a Gold Medallist of the Royal College of Music, where his teachers included John Barstow and Kendall Taylor. His studies were continued with Paul Badura-Skoda in Germany. Since his debút in 1974 he has toured widely in Europe, Africa and the United States. Simon Nicholls has made a special study of Scriabin, on whose music he has given lecture-recitals, broadcasts and published articles. His other publications include *The Young Cellist's Repertoire* (Faber), in collaboration with Julian Lloyd-Webber. Simon Nicholls teaches piano at the Yehudi Menuhin School and is a Professor at the Royal College of Music.

Sir Sacheverell Sitwell, Bart., was born in Scarborough in 1897 and educated at Eton College. A prolific author, chiefly of poetry and works on the arts, architecture and travel, his first book (of poetry) was published in 1918 and his latest, *An*

Indian Summer, consisting of one hundred poems, was published in 1982. Sir Sacheverell has written biographies of Mozart, Liszt and Offenbach and is Vice-President of the Liszt Society. He was made a Companion of Honour in 1984.

Ronald Stevenson studied at the Royal Manchester College of Music and the Academia Nazionale di Santa Cecilia in Rome. As a virtuoso pianist, broadcaster and lecturer, he is particularly associated with his own music and that of Busoni and Percy Grainger, of which he has recently recorded examples on the *Altarus* label. His career has taken him to all the continents except South America and a more recent tour of the Far East included performances and composition seminars at the University of Shanghai. His many and varied compositions range from songs, of which there are now over three hundred, to the monumental *Passacaglia on DSCH* for solo piano. Amongst his commissioned works are his *Second Piano Concerto* (for the BBC 'Proms'), a song cycle, *Border Boyhood* for Peter Pears and a *Violin Concerto* for Yehudi Menuhin. Ronald Stevenson's literary output includes *Western Music – an introduction* (Kahn and Averill 1971), articles for *The Listener* and other periodicals, and many radio and television scripts, but his *magnum opus* in this field is a massive biography of Ferrucio Busoni, which has yet to be published.

Harold Taylor studied at the Royal Manchester College of Music, Goldsmith's College, London and with Raymond Thiberge and Alfred Cortot in Paris. He was Artistic Director of the Bromsgrove Festival from 1966 until 1980 and Head of Music at North Worcestershire College until 1982. He now teaches privately in London. Harold Taylor is the author of *The Pianist's Talent* (Kahn and Averill 1979).

Romi Tunstall-Behrens lives and paints in Cornwall – on the opposite coast from St. Ives. Her portraits include many of the distinguished artists who have taught at the International Musicians' Seminar at nearby Prussia Cove and she has exhibited in Bristol and London.

Marguerite Wolff began formal study of the piano with her mother at the age of five. She gave her first Wigmore Hall recital when she was ten, made her concerto debút under Sir John Barbirolli five years later, and was appointed to the teaching staff of Trinity College, London, at the age of twenty-one. She has toured the Far East and South America as well as Europe and the USA. In addition to the music of Chopin and Liszt, Marguerite Wolff has a special affinity with that of Sir Arthur Bliss. She was the first pianist to record his *Piano Sonata* and gave the first performance of his *Wedding Suite*. Marguerite Wolff is a member of the Council of the Liszt Society.